Sergei Tchoban

Art

Sergei Tchoban

Art

images
Publishing

Published in Australia in 2010 by
The Images Publishing Group Pty Ltd
ABN 89 059 734 431
6 Bastow Place, Mulgrave, Victoria 3170, Australia
Tel: +61 3 9561 5544 Fax: +61 3 9561 4860
books@imagespublishing.com
www.imagespublishing.com

Copyright © The Images Publishing Group Pty Ltd 2010
The Images Publishing Group Reference Number: 926

National Library of Australia Cataloguing-in-Publication entry:

Author:	Tchoban, Sergei, 1962-
Title:	Sergei Tchoban : art / Sergei Tchoban.
Edition:	1st ed.
ISBN:	9781864703894 (hbk.)
Notes:	Includes index.
Subjects:	Tchoban, Sergei, 1962-
	Architecture–Europe.
	Architectural drawing–Europe.
Dewey Number:	720.92

Designed by The Graphic Image Studio Pty Ltd, Mulgrave, Australia
www.tgis.com.au

Pre-publishing services by United Graphic Pte Ltd, Singapore

Printed on 157gsm GoldEast Matt Art by Everbest Printing Co. Ltd., Hong Kong/China

Contents

REALITY IS TRUTH, ART IS BEAUTY

Sergei Tchoban, Dreaming-onto-paper

By Kevin Nance

Drawing was once essential to the architect. From Palladio to Frank Lloyd Wright, pen and paper were the fundamental tools for learning, dreaming and visualizing. Just as student painters once taught themselves by copying the Old Masters, their counterparts in architecture sketched the buildings they admired, a process that trained both hand and eye, feeding their technical skills and imaginations. Wright honed his talent as a designer by working as a draftsman for Louis Sullivan, himself no slouch with charcoal and parchment. Even now, a quarter-century into the age of the pixel, a few diehards (Renzo Piano, Santiago Calatrava) persist in developing their ideas primarily in analog form—doodles morphing into abstract or evocative shapes and, finally, into buildings. But in this age of computer-aided design, the hand of the architect is fast becoming atrophied. You use it or lose it; many are losing it. The earliest hand-drawn sketches in architecture firms today are quickly scanned and imported into 3-D programs such as AutoCAD and Rhino, after which typically there's no need to develop the sketches further as inspiration or illustration, let alone as works of art in their own right.

Which brings us to Sergei Tchoban. The Russian artist-architect, who was born in St. Petersburg and has lived and worked in Germany since the early 1990s, has wielded the pen and pencil with a level of skill, concentration, creative intention and diversity of purpose that may be unparalleled in his generation. While not technically an autodidact–he was formally schooled in his hometown–Tchoban clearly pursued the drawing of buildings from the first as a means of self-education in perspective, proportion and the Vitruvian virtues of commodity, firmness and delight. And yet the object of this education, also from the start, has been to prepare him for far more than visualizing his own buildings. For Tchoban, architectural drawing is both process and product, a means to an end and an end in itself.

Endings, of course, are also beginnings. As demonstrated by the hauntingly beautiful drawings in this book, Tchoban has spent much of his adult life looking at architecture around the world, at times with eyes wide open, at other times squinting a bit, letting the image blur, warp, transform. The drawings are alternately (and sometimes simultaneously) precise and notional–starting points, in both cases,

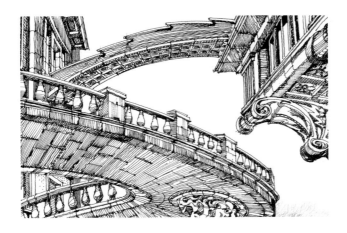

for imaginative exploration. Buildings function for Tchoban as crucibles of beauty, as objects of desire and fascination, and, most powerfully, as talismans with which he focuses and channels his creative energy into intuitive and sometimes mystical realms. As in the work of Surrealists from Dali to Remedios Varo, the architectures of the past (especially in classical, Gothic and Baroque modes) are often for Tchoban portals into an array of alternate urban realities that feel like near relatives of those described by a fictional Marco Polo in Calvino's *Invisible Cities*. Tchoban's head-tripping fantasias of formal and spatial relationships, with their networks of connecting stairways and corridors (as in *Vertical composition of bridges and stairs, infinitely growing*, from 2009), recall those of M.C. Escher. Tchoban is at once a throwback and a futurist, forever introducing yesterday to tomorrow, creating a world that is not timeless but, rather, straddles epochs. One of the most poignant images here is his *View across the Neva River to Smolnij Monastery in Saint Petersburg*, from 1985, with a grim modern building in the right foreground seeming to lean toward, even yearn for, the domed splendor in the distance. If the building in the

foreground could speak, we feel, it would do so in the voice of Sergei Tchoban. And that voice would be full of awe.

There's a romantic, even Gothic atmosphere about much of the work. The view of a Russian born in the Soviet Union and now living in Germany, even half a century past the events of World War II, will naturally be composed of particular colors–those of smoke and ashes (and, conveniently, charcoal and India ink). Even the earliest drawings in this book are often startlingly moody, the buildings hunkered down beneath glowering, suffocating skies, like Poe's tenebrous House of Usher. We feel, in some of the early views of St. Petersburg, a Slavic melancholy of the sort associated with Pushkin and Dostoyevsky. These are the wintry streets of Eugene Onegin, of Raskolnikov, and later of Lenin–who eventually appears, wittily and yet somehow sorrowfully, in Tchoban's fanciful designs for buildings in the form of the Soviet hero's fallen, hollowed-out statues. (In other times and places, Tchoban might have become a celebrated illustrator of books by Dickens or Baudelaire, or a darkly satirical postmodern filmmaker along the lines of Tim Burton.) And yet this

crepuscular emotional weather travels well. It follows Tchoban almost everywhere he goes, from Paris and Prague to Spain and Italy, like a thundercloud carrying with it the permanent threat of rain.

At times the rain leads to flooding. Perhaps the single most striking aspect of this book is the frequency and intensity with which Tchoban returns to a vision of cities on (and often under) water. Sometimes these aquatic cityscapes are more or less realistic, depicting or inspired by Venice, which we might reasonably guess to be the artist's urban ideal. (He visits the Las Vegas version as well as the real thing, perhaps bemused–but hardly appalled–by the former and ravished by the latter; the Rialto Bridge, which holds particular fascination perhaps because of its Escher-like properties, shows up on both occasions.) In the "Water Worlds" series here (1995), and in images of St. Petersburg and other real and imagined cities largely submerged by some thousand-year deluge (or perhaps by the rising oceans predicted by some as the catastrophic byproduct of global warming), Tchoban's dreaming-onto-paper finds its most lyrical, mysterious and affecting form. Among the many surprises in these diluvial vistas is the fact that they're

far from apocalyptic; there are no drowning bodies, no evidence of the damage to buildings one might expect in an actual flood. If anything, these snow-globe scenes are seductive, serene and vaguely utopian–far more appealing, come to think of it, than many of the "real" cityscapes elsewhere in the book. Collectively they conjure a new avatar of the lost continent of Atlantis; all you'd need for a perfect night out would be a gondola, a picnic basket and the moon overhead.

It's striking, too, how little Tchoban's imagination, at least as expressed in the drawings, seems drawn to the more spartan forms of modernism. The legacy of the Bauhaus and Mies van der Rohe is not much in evidence here; on the historical continuum of architecture, Tchoban's capacity for celebration seems to stall just past Art Nouveau. If reality is truth and art is beauty, as in the title of one of the artist's most enigmatic watercolors from 2002, Tchoban seems to favor art and beauty (as exemplified by Beaux Arts motifs) over reality and truth (of the sort embodied in buildings of the more recent past and present). Frank Lloyd Wright would not have approved, but no matter. Tchoban is enamored of and inspired by

vaulted ceilings, coffered soffits, terraced setbacks, patterned fenestration, arches, domes, spires, finials, buttresses, bell towers, cupolas, rotundas, great stone plazas and town squares anchored by monumental civic sculpture. When he sketches designs for contemporary projects, such as the Tresor Club on the Spree River (2003) or the Templehof Airfield (2008), it's with a sense of rightness, and a certain inevitability, that these manage to suggest the Piazza San Marco and the Doge's Palace. There are occasional attempts, albeit speculative, to marry modern design with the glorious past; see his *Urban maritime vision with Palladian and modern motifs* (1992), his contemporary vision of the Ponte Vecchio as a crazy quilt of interlocking rectangular masses (1999), and his sketch of a museum tower of stacked boxes (2010), this last perhaps intentionally reminiscent of New York's New Museum, jauntily (and perhaps defiantly) ornamented with a découpage of Baroque architectural detail.

For the architecturally oriented reader, especially one with an historical or scholarly bent, this book of course contains much fodder for thought. But the general art-loving reader, unburdened by professional considerations and perhaps too many layers of educated perspective, may in the end be better off. Certainly the pleasure in these pages is as abundant and uncomplicated as we choose to make it.

The best plan, probably, is simply to follow Tchoban, a modern-day Marco Polo, on his travels, seeing what he sees. After this bracing voyage, the reader might find it worth his or her while to take a second pass through, this time noticing how Tchoban frames what he sees–what he chooses to show and, perhaps just as important, what he leaves out. Of particular note in this regard is the "Polyptych" series of urban scenes framed by windows (2009), which is as revealing as anything here about Tchoban's vision. In these poignantly circumscribed views through apertures in cracked plaster walls that are all too real and all too true, we glimpse with Tchoban what art and beauty look like, and lean toward them, yearning.

Kevin Nance is a Chicago-based writer and editor. He is the former art and architecture critic for the Chicago Sun-Times, *and has also written for* ARTnews, Art in America, Art & Auction, Poets & Writers, *and other publications.*

S e r g e i   T c h o b a n
Works of Art

Old Russian town, 1979
21 x 30 cm, watercolor

Old Russian town, 1979
30 x 21 cm, colored pencil

Tchernyshov Bridge, Saint Petersburg, 1979
21 x 17 cm, charcoal

Rostov the Great, 1979
24 x 16 cm, Indian ink

Tallin, 1979
24 x 37 cm, charcoal

Tallin, 1979
36 x 24 cm, charcoal

Staircase at 4 Dimitrovsky Alley, Saint Petersburg, 1979
45 x 34 cm, watercolor

Tchernyshov Bridge, Saint Petersburg, 1982
24 x 34 cm, watercolor

Prague, 1984
30 x 46 cm, charcoal

Prague, 1984
31 x 30 cm, pencil

Prague, 1984
45 x 30 cm, charcoal

Prague, 1984
30 x 45 cm, colored pencil

Prague, 1984
27 x 39 cm, watercolor, Indian ink

Backyard in Saint Petersburg, 1984
47 x 30 cm, Indian ink, watercolor

25

View across the Neva River to Smolnij Monastery in Saint Petersburg, 1985
31 x 44 cm, charcoal

Courtyard view from the Saint Petersburg apartment, 1985
37 x 26 cm, charcoal

Firewall on Dimitrovski Alley, 1985
34 x 47 cm, watercolor

Belfry of Prince Vladimir Church, Saint Petersburg, 1987
46 x 22 cm, pastel

Interior detail of the Saint Petersburg television tower, 1989
78 x 58 cm, pencil, watercolor

The Russian Fashion Building, with hotel, 1989
33 x 24 cm, pencil, watercolor

Draft for a waterfront area in Saint Petersburg, 1989
48 x 70 cm, pencil, watercolor

House at Vladmirski Square, Saint Petersburg, 1989
35 x 45 cm, watercolor

Monmartre, Paris, 1990
36 x 26 cm, Indian ink, watercolor

Café Le Consulat, 1990
18 x 28 cm, Indian ink, watercolor

Paris, 1990
40 x 30 cm, Indian ink, watercolor

Church space in Paris, 1990
32 x 22 cm, Indian ink, watercolor

Roman Impression, 1992
62 x 44 cm, construction paper, charcoal, chalk

Trajan's Forum in Rome, 1992
44 x 62 cm, Indian ink, watercolor

Old Town passage in Rome, 1992
59 x 42 cm, construction paper, charcoal, chalk

Urban maritime vision with Palladian and modern motifs, 1992
65 x 47 cm, charcoal

High-rise buildings at Columbus Circle in New York City, 1992
42   63 x 45 cm, Indian ink, watercolor

Toronto, 1992
44 x 32 cm, charcoal

Toronto, 1992
44 x 32 cm, charcoal

Dome relics, 1993
19 x 52 cm, pastel

Architectural study, 1994
41 x 45 cm, pencil

Composite picture of Dresden's Frauenkirche, 1994
55 x 44 cm, pencil, watercolor

Lenin from above and below, 1994
34 x 34 cm, Indian ink, watercolor

Space study for the transept of Leipzig central station, 1994
34 x 34 cm, Indian ink, watercolor

Prague, 1994
41 x 31 cm, Indian ink

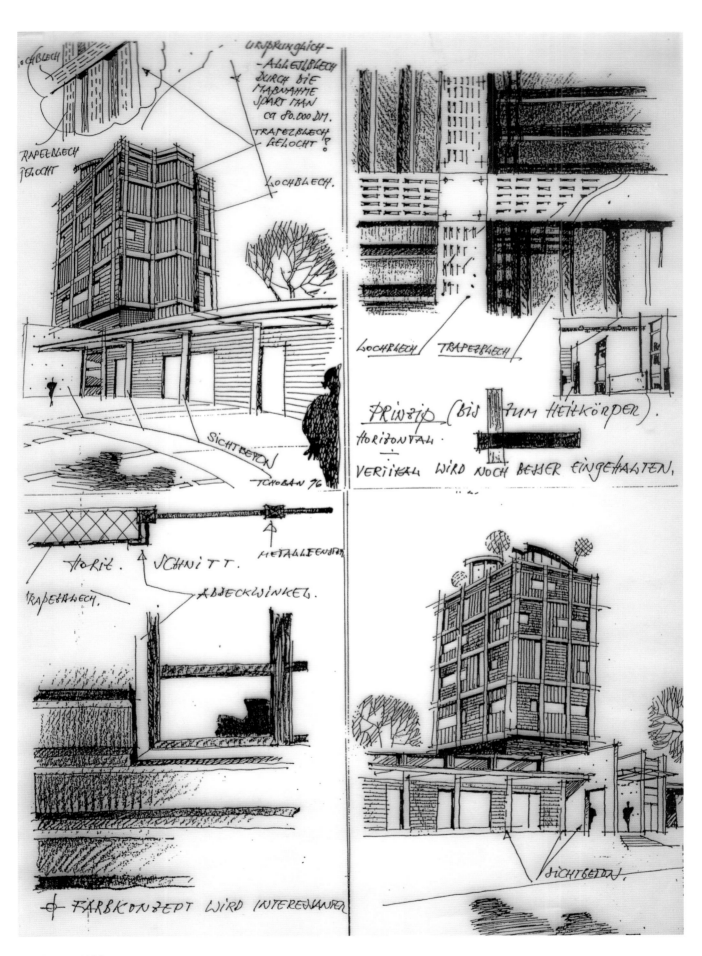

Java Tower, 1995
42 x 30 cm, Indian ink

Water worlds 1, 1995
37 x 32 cm, Indian ink, watercolor

Water worlds 2, 1995
36 x 32 cm, Indian ink

Water worlds 3, 1995
32 x 37 cm, Indian ink, watercolor

Water worlds 4, 1995
37 x 32 cm, Indian ink, watercolor

Rising waters, 1996
48 x 46 cm, Indian ink, watercolor

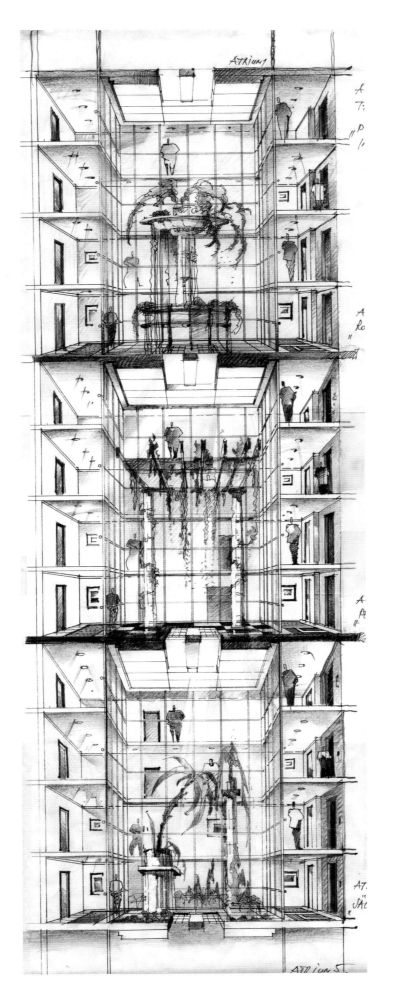

Atrium of the high-rise building at Sternplatz in Potsdam, 1996
73 x 28 cm, pencil, felt-tip pen

Java Tower staircase draft, 1996
70 x 44 cm, colored pencil and felt-tip pen on a blueprint

Sterncenter, 1996
21 x 29 cm, Indian ink, colored pencil

Caprice on the architectural furore of feverish baroque spatial fantasies, 1997
28 x 26 cm, Indian ink, watercolor

Caprice on the architectural furore of feverish Baroque spatial fantasies, 1997
29 x 28 cm, Indian ink, watercolor

New study on the relationship between water and architecture, 1997
44 x 46 cm, Indian ink, watercolor

Study for "Simple Forms" (San Francesco in Pienza), 1998
32 x 32 cm, Indian ink

Arndt Gallery, 1998
21 x 29 cm, felt-tip pen, tracing paper

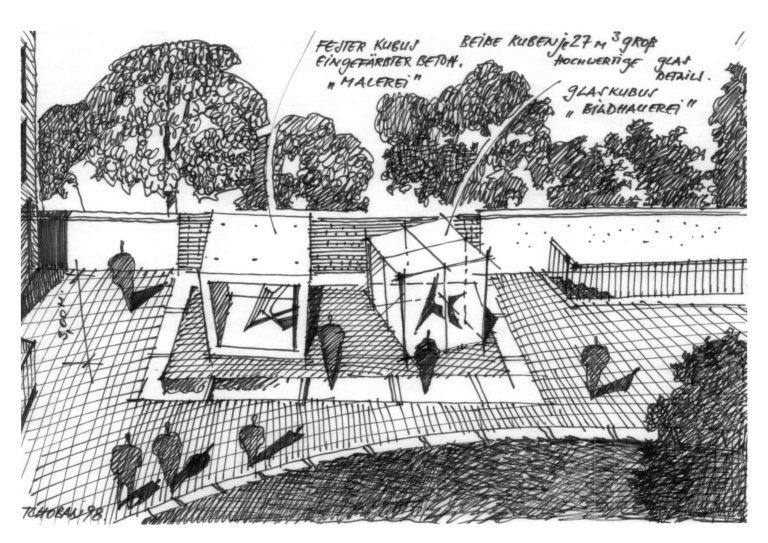

Arndt Gallery, 1998
21 x 29 cm, felt-tip pen, tracing paper

Courtyard of the Tacheles Quarter in Berlin, seen as a theater scene, 1999
24 x 100 cm, Indian ink, watercolor

Simple forms, 1998
66 x 46 cm, Indian ink, watercolor

Ponte Vecchio 1, 1998
45 x 65 cm, Indian ink, watercolor

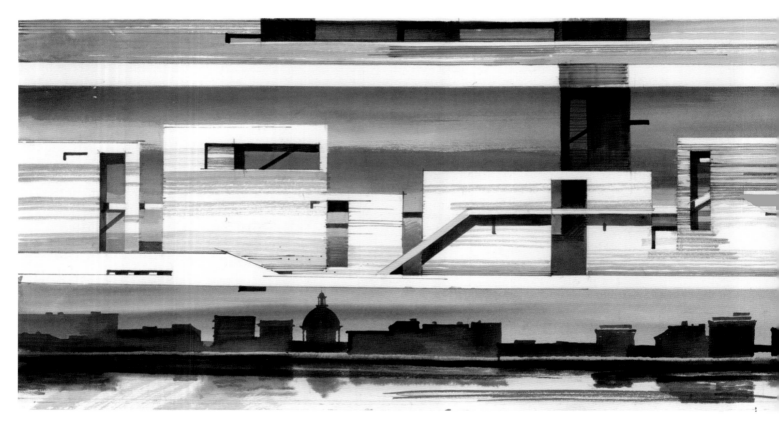

Modern Ponte Vecchio, 1999
34 x 100 cm, Indian ink, watercolor

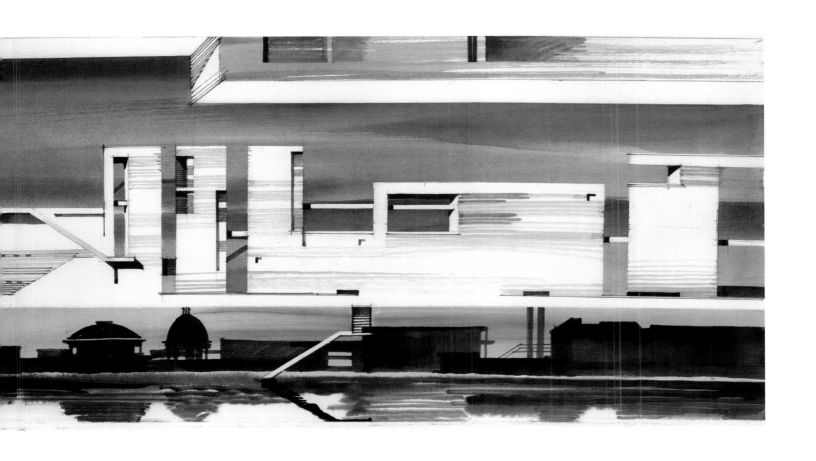

Old and new street façade in Johannisviertel, Berlin, connected with transparent bridges I, 1999
24 x 100 cm, Indian ink, watercolor

Old and new street façade in Johannisviertel, Berlin, connected with transparent bridges II, 1999
24 x 100 cm, Indian ink, watercolor

Old and new street façade in Johannisviertel, Berlin, connected with transparent bridges III, 1999
24 x 100 cm, Indian ink, watercolor

Draft for the Egyptian embassy, 1999
16 x 16 cm, pencil, colored pencil

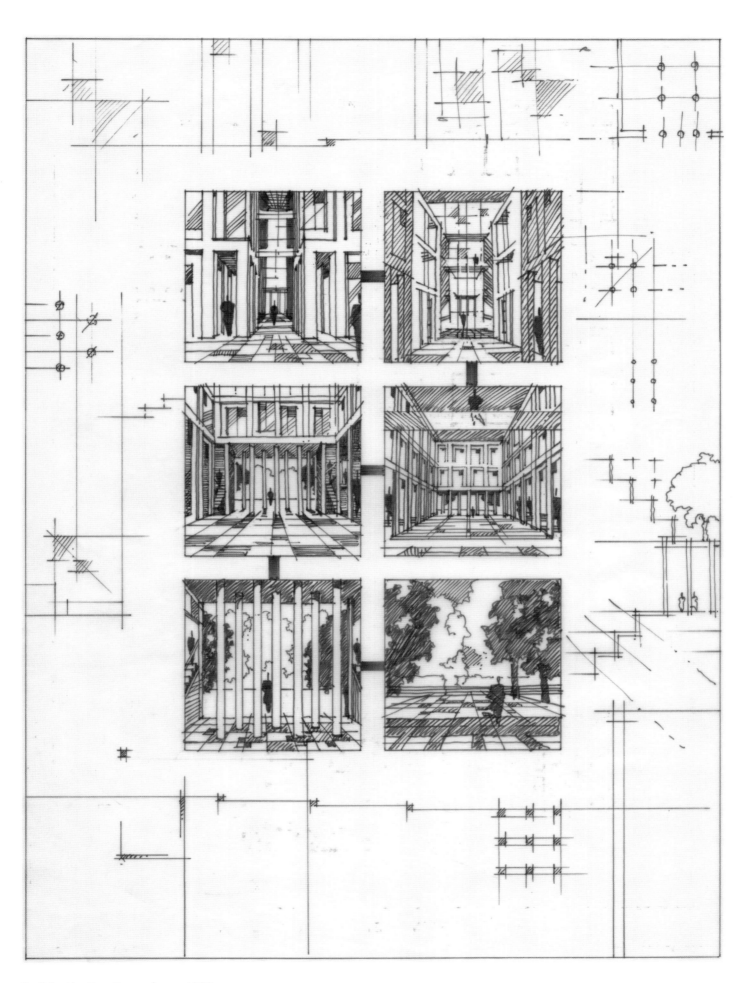

Draft for the Egyptian embassy, 1999
38 x 28 cm, felt-tip pen

Study for the pavilion of the Aedes Gallery, 1999
24 x 100 cm, Indian ink, watercolor

Backyard studies of the Johannis Quarter, 1999
59 x 58 cm, Indian ink, watercolor

Sunken church, 2000
29 x 20 cm, watercolor

Lock of the Moskva–Volga Canal I, 2001
35 x 56 cm, Indian ink, watercolor

Lock of the Moskva—Volga Canal II, 2001
35 x 56 cm, Indian ink, watercolor

Lock of the Moskva–Volga Canal III, 2001
55 x 37 cm, Indian ink, watercolor

Lock of the Moskva–Volga Canal IV, 2001
54 x 34 cm, Indian ink, watercolor

Two fluids, two realities, 2001
60 x 43 cm, Indian ink, watercolor

Underwater settlement, 2002
40 x 14 cm, pencil, felt-tip pen, colored pencil, Indian ink

Reality is Truth, Art is Beauty, 2002
56 x 39 cm, Indian ink, watercolour

Diary pages, 2002
27 x 38 cm, pencil, felt-tip pen, colored pencil, ink

Diary pages, 2002
38 x 27 cm, pencil, felt-tip pen, colored pencil, ink

Diary pages, 2002
39 x 27 cm, pencil, felt-tip pen, colored pencil, ink

Diary sketches, 2002
17 x 20 cm, Indian ink, colored pencil

Underwater scenario on the pages of a trashy novel, 2002
17 x 10 cm, felt-tip pen, pencil

Draft of tower buildings at the Lehrter Bahnhof train station, 2002
54 x 37 cm, Indian ink, watercolor

Tresor Club on the Spree River, 2003
26 x 19 cm, pencil

Tresor Club on the Spree River, 2003
18 x 26 cm, pencil

Tresor Club on the Spree River, 2003
18 x 26 cm, pencil

Tresor Club on the Spree River, 2003
18 x 26 cm, pencil

Tresor Club on the Spree River, 2003
18 x 26 cm, pencil

Tresor Club on the Spree River, 2003
18 x 26 cm, pencil

Variant of the Tresor Club, 2003
33 x 45 cm, charcoal, watercolor

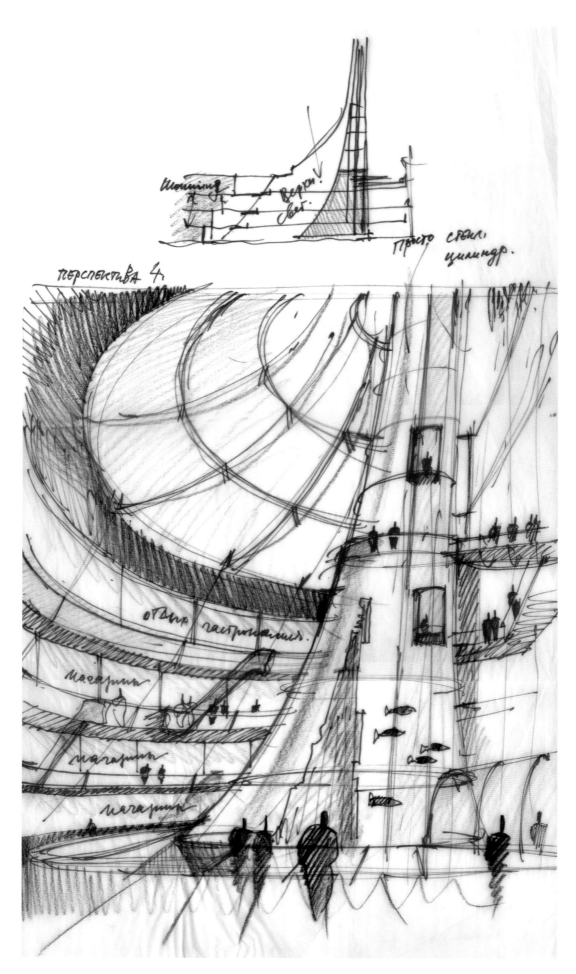

Foyer, Federation Tower, 2003
63 x 33 cm, pencil, felt-tip pen, colored pencil

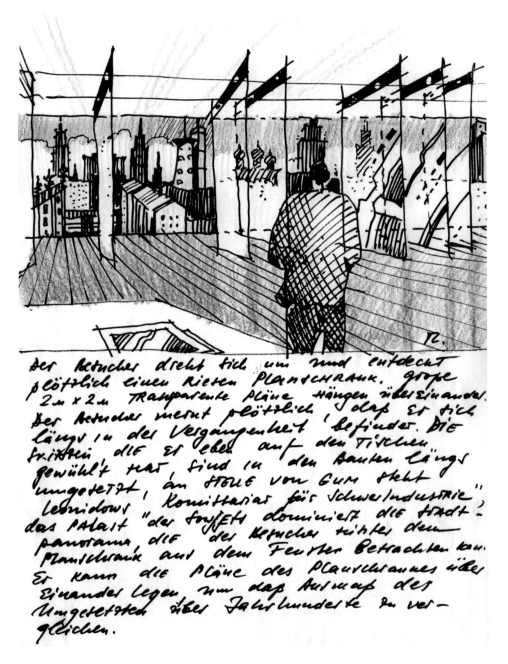

Der Betrachter dreht sich um und entdeckt
plötzlich einen Riesen Planschrank. große
2m x 2m Transparente Pläne hängen übereinander.
Der Betrachter merkt plötzlich, daß er sich
längs in der Vergangenheit befindet. DIE
Schritten die er eben auf den Tischen
gewühlt hat, sind in den Bauten längs
umgesetzt, an Stelle von GUM steht
Leonidows "Komissariat für Schwerindustrie"
das Palais der Sowjets dominiert die Stadt -
panorama, die der Betrachter hinter dem
Planschrank aus dem Fenster betrachten kan.
Er kann die Pläne des Planschrankes über
einander legen, um das Ausmaß des
Umgesetzten über Jahrhunderte zu ver -
gleichen.

Sketches for the exhibition "STADTanSICHTEN –
Planschrank Moskau: Ort einer Hauptstadt", 2003
29 x 21 cm, Indian ink, colored pencil

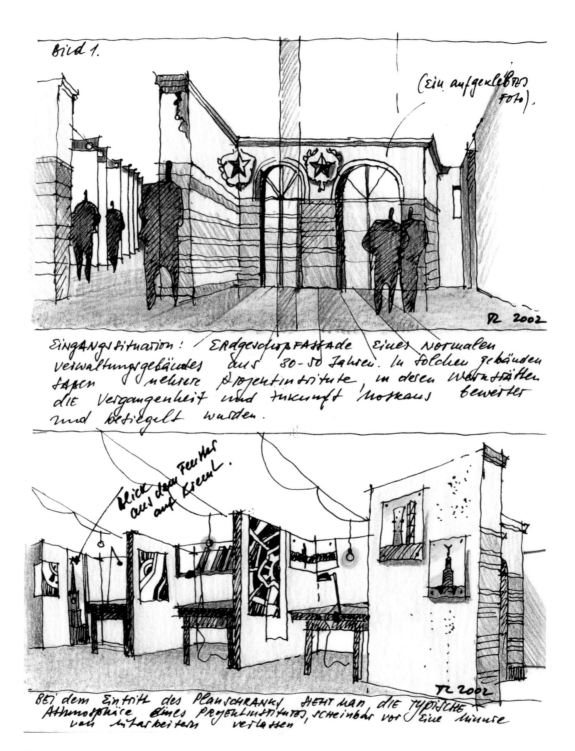

Sketches for the exhibition "STADTanSICHTEN – Planschrank Moskau: Ort einer Hauptstadt", 2003
29 x 21 cm, Indian ink

Staging for the exhibition "STADTanSICHTEN – Planschrank Moskau: Ort einer Hauptstadt", 2003
21 x 29 cm, felt-tip pen, colored pencil

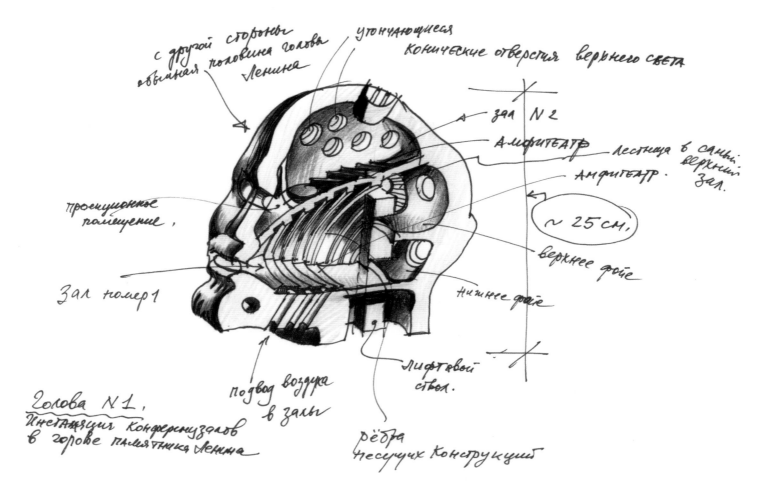

с другой стороны
обычная половина голова
Ленина

утончающиеся

конические отверстия верхнего света

зал N 2

Амфитеатр

лестница в самы
верхний
зал.

Амфитеатр.

~ 25 см.

верхнее фойе

проигцияние
помещение ,

нижнее фойе

Зал номер 1

лифтовой
ствол.

подвод воздуха
в залы

рёбра
несущих конструкций

Голова N 1.
Инстаняция конференузалов
в голове памятника Ленина

Architectural fantasy: Lenin, 2003
21 x 29 cm, Indian ink, colored pencil

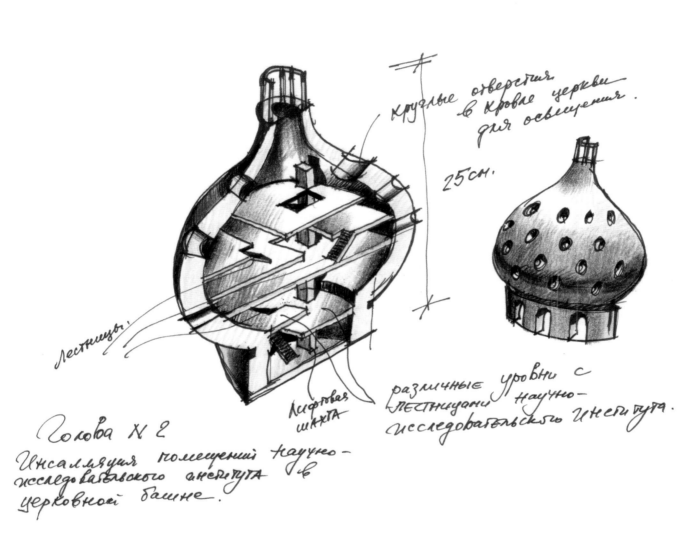

круглые отверстия
в кровле церкви
для освещения.

25см.

лестницы.

Лифтовая
шахта

различные уровни с
лестницами научно-
исследовательского института.

Голова № 2
Инсталляция помещений научно-
исследовательского института в
церковной башне.

Architectural fantasy: Tower, 2003
21 x 29 cm, Indian ink

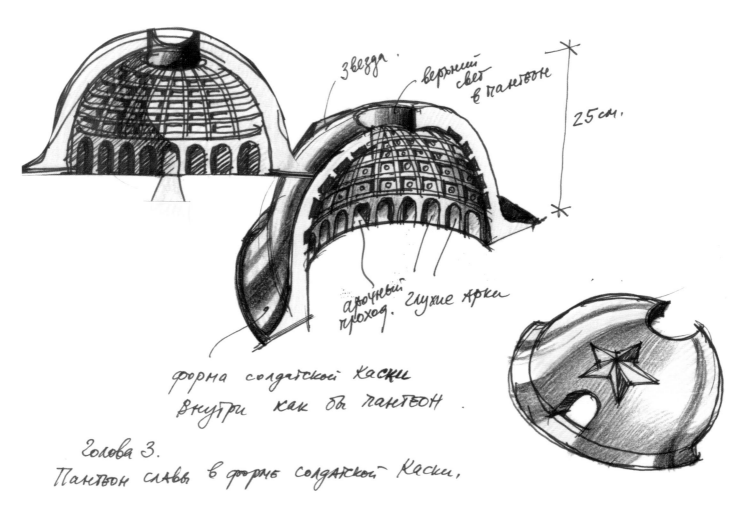

звезда.

верхний свет в пантеон

25см.

арочный проход. Глухие Арки

форма солдатской Каски
Внутри как бы пантеон.

Голова 3.
Пантеон славы в форме солдатской Каски.

Architectural fantasy: Helmet, 2003
21 x 29 cm, Indian ink, colored pencil

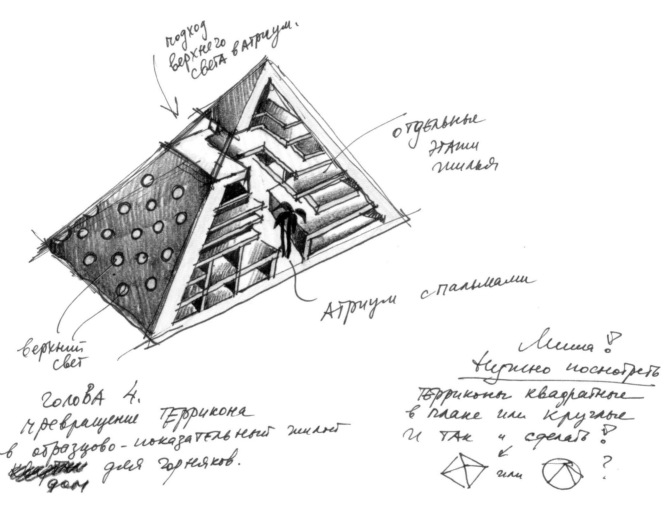

Architectural fantasy: Pyramid, 2003
21 x 29 cm, Indian ink, colored pencil

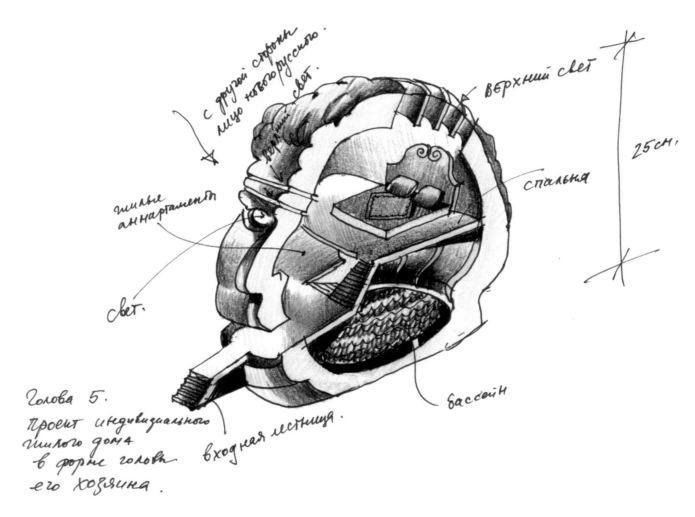

с другой стороны
лицо нового русского.

верхний свет

верхний свет

25см.

спальня

жилые
аппартаменты

свет.

бассейн

Голова 5.
Проект индивидуального
жилого дома
в форме головы   входная лестница.
его хозяина.

Architectural fantasy: New Russian, 2003
21 x 29 cm, Indian ink, colored pencil

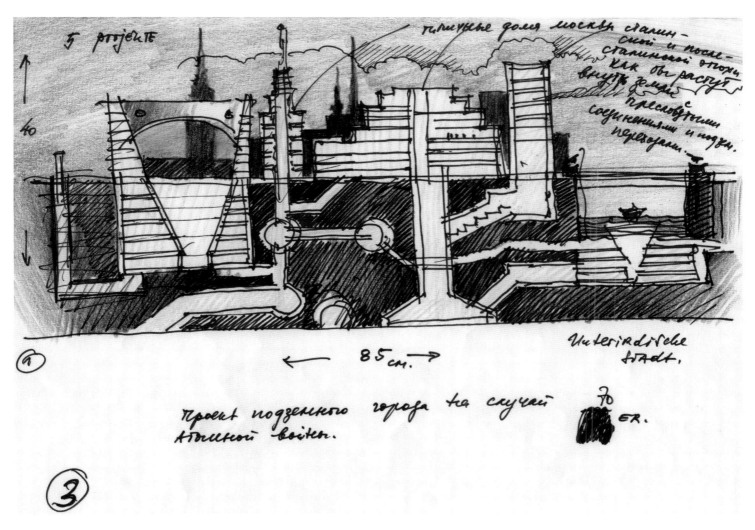

Moscow excavated, 2003
21 x 30 cm, pencil, felt-tip pen, colored pencil

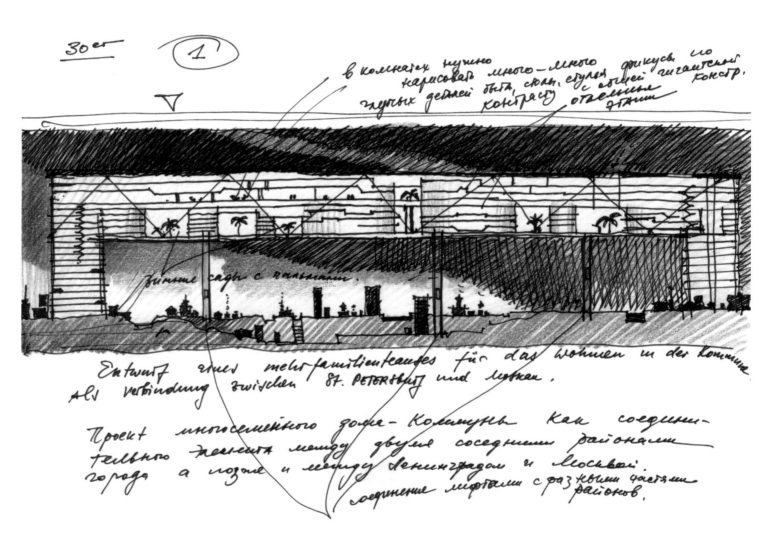

Architectural fantasy: City Bridge, 2003
21 x 29 cm, pencil, felt-tip pen, colored pencil

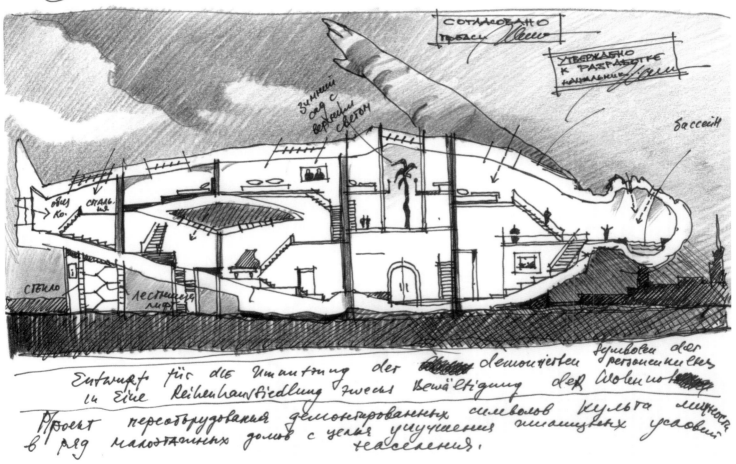

Architectural fantasy: Fallen Statue, 2003
21 x 29 cm, Indian ink, colored pencil

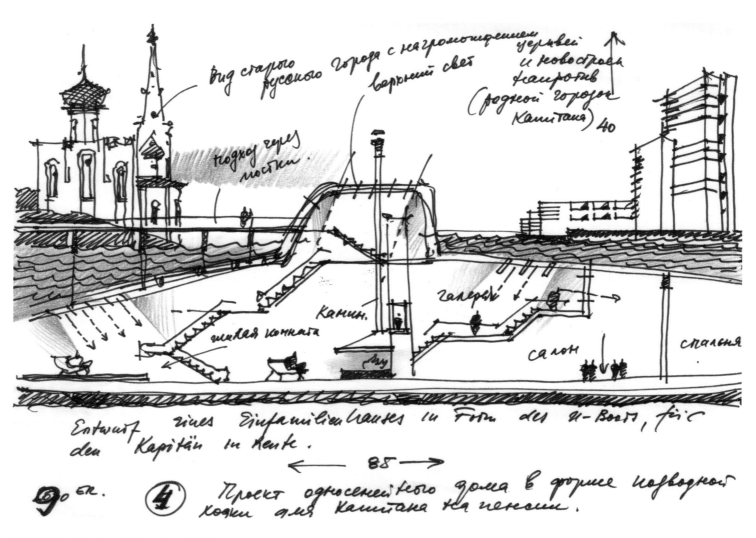

Architectural fantasy: Submarine, 2003
21 x 29 cm, Indian ink, colored pencil

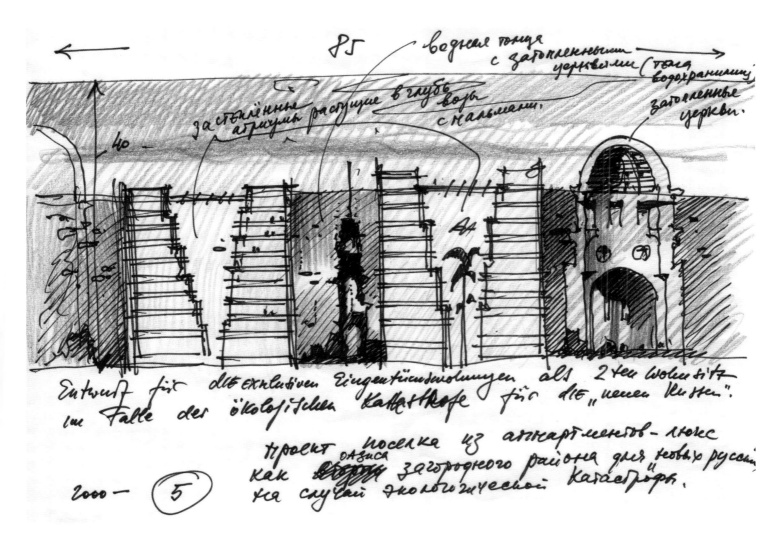

Architectural fantasy: Subterranean City, 2003
21 x 29 cm, Indian ink, colored pencil

Moscow, the underground city, protected from the atom bomb, 2003
21 x 30 cm, felt-tip pen, pencil

Architectural fantasy: Lenin's head, 2003
21 x 17 cm, felt-tip pen, pencil

Greek church with dome, 2004
26 x 31 cm, charcoal

Precious spoils, 2004
21 x 29 cm, charcoal

Lungarno Corsini, Florence, 2004
37 x 56 cm, Indian ink, watercolor

Piazza del Duomo, Pistoia, 2004
56 x 37 cm, Indian ink, watercolor

Women bathing at the Hotel Bellagio, Las Vegas, 2004
31 x 56 cm, pastel

The Venetian in Las Vegas, 2004
42 x 56 cm, pastel

Interstices, 2004
13 x 13 cm x 3, pastel

Venetian mirror, 2004
25 x 33 cm, pastel

The snow-covered historic city becomes a mythical place beneath water level, 2004
42 x 42 cm, pastel

Three dresses, 2004
40 x 60 cm, pastel

Baroque city in the water, 2004
30 x 41 cm, Indian ink, watercolor

Dance theatre for Boris Eifman, 2005
21 x 30 cm, colored pencil, pencil

Dance theatre for Boris Eifman, 2005
21 x 30 cm, colored pencil, pencil

Dance theatre for Boris Eifman, 2005
30 x 42 cm, Indian ink, colored pencil

Saint Petersburg dream II, 2005
30 x 40 cm, charcoal, watercolor

Five corners (sketch), 2005
19 x 12 cm, charcoal

Saint Petersburg dream I: Five corners, 2005
40 x 28 cm, charcoal, watercolor

White Nights of Saint Petersburg, 2005
44 x 61 cm, charcoal, watercolor

New York City, 2005
56 x 35 cm, pastel

Courtyard in Montecatini Terme, 2005
32 x 41 cm, pencil, pastel, watercolor

House on the island of Majorca, 2005
55 x 39 cm, pastel

Ancient ruins in Turkey, 2005
30 x 21 cm, pastel

Ancient ruins in Turkey, 2005
21 x 30 cm, pastel

Клуб на 300 мест   С Чобан 2005

Function hall for 200 persons, 2005
50 x 65 cm, pastel

Venice, drowning pictures, 2006
59 x 42 cm, charcoal

The Pantheon, Rome, 2006
53 x 72 cm, watercolor, Indian ink

Italian cityscape, 2006
42 x 60 cm, Indian ink, watercolor

Piazza San Pietro, Rome, 2006
53 x 72 cm, watercolor, Indian ink

Piazza Venezia, Rome, 2006
52 x 72 cm, watercolor, Indian ink

La Giralda in Seville, 2006
38 x 55 cm, Indian ink, watercolor

Cathedral of Malaga, 2006
60 x 39 cm, Indian ink, watercolor

151

Cathedral of Amalfi, 2006
40 x 32 cm, pastel

Granada, 2006
57 x 39 cm, pastel

Garden in Marbella, 2006
33 x 50 cm, gouache, watercolor

Evening in Positano, 2006
40 x 32 cm, pastel

Marbella, 2006
56 x 29 cm, watercolor

Napoli, 2006
40 x 32 cm, pastel

Backyard in Sorrento, 2006
60 x 40 cm, pastel

Parisian architectural fantasy, 2006
42 x 59 cm, pastel

Sorrento, 2006
40 x 32 cm, pastel

Preparatory drawing for the porch design of the Axel-Springer-Strasse office
building, 2006
29 x 18 cm, pencil, watercolor

Architectural fantasy on the Dubinivskaya Street office complex, Moscow, 2007
65 x 50 cm, charcoal

Saint Petersburg courtyard, 2007
42 x 24 cm, Indian ink, watercolor

Saint Petersburg fantasy, 2007
43 x 65 cm, watercolor, charcoal

Out of the window, 2007
56 x 37 cm, watercolor

White Nights 2, 2007
40 x 30 cm, charcoal

White Nights 1, 2007
30 x 40 cm, charcoal

White Nights 4, 2007
30 x 40 cm, charcoal

White Nights 3, 2007
30 x 40 cm, charcoal

White nights of Saint Petersburg, 2007
54 x 76 cm, pastel

Conservatorium in Budapest, 2007
37 x 57 cm, charcoal, watercolor

Seu de Palma, Cathedral of Palma de Mallorca, 2007
42 x 52 cm, chalk, black paper

Seu de Palma, Cathedral of Palma de Mallorca, 2007
67 x 41 cm, pastel

Seu de Palma, Cathedral of Palma de Mallorca, 2007
67 x 41 cm, Indian ink, watercolor

Seu de Palma, Cathedral of Palma de Mallorca, 2007
67 x 41 cm, charcoal

Seu de Palma, Cathedral of Palma de Mallorca, 2007
67 x 41 cm, Indian ink, watercolor

Girona, 2008
38 x 55 cm, watercolor

Catalonia, 2008
54 x 35 cm, watercolor, Indian ink

Catalonia, 2008
35 x 54 cm, watercolor, Indian ink

Catalonia, 2008
34 x 25 cm, charcoal

Old town in Catalonia, 2008
25 x 34 cm, charcoal

Catalonia, 2008
25 x 34 cm, charcoal

Catalonia, 2008
25 x 34 cm, charcoal

Taormina, Sicily, 2008
33 x 25 cm, charcoal

Taormina, Sicily, 2008
33 x 25 cm, charcoal

Taormina, Sicily, 2008
39 x 59 cm, watercolor, Indian ink

Saint Petersburg courtyard near the Vladimir belfry, 2008
30 x 40 cm, watercolor, pencil

St. Nicolas Cathedral and belfry, 2008
30 x 40 cm, watercolor, pencil

Art nouveau houses near Vladimir Square, 2008
40 x 30 cm, watercolor, pencil

Aura, 2008
26 x 40 cm, pencil, felt-tip pen on tracing paper

Aura, 2008
26 x 40 cm, pencil, felt-tip pen on tracing paper

Aqua (sketch), 2008
21 x 15 cm, pencil

Aqua, 2008
27 x 19 cm, pencil

Waterside city, 2008
30 x 21 cm, ballpoint pen

Temple in the water, 2008
19 x 27 cm, pencil

Federation Island in Sochi: square, 2008
19 x 27 cm, pencil

Federation Island in Sochi: promenade, 2008
19 x 27cm, pencil

Draft for a Villa on Bettinastrasse, 2008
42 x 30 cm, pencil

Federation Island in Sochi, 2008
19 x 27 cm, pencil

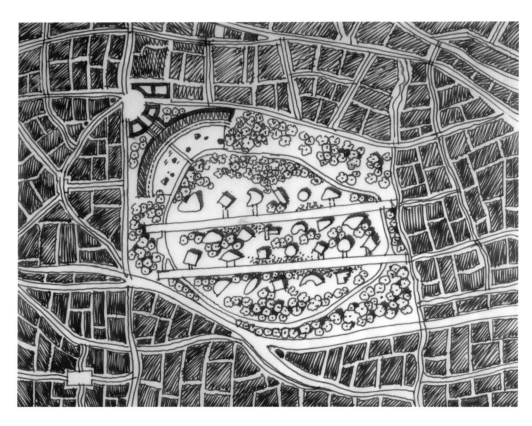

Tempelhof airfield, 2008
28 x 35 cm, Indian ink

Tempelhof airfield, 2008
38 x 56 cm, watercolor

Tempelhof airfield, 2008
39 x 56 cm, watercolor, Indian ink

Tempelhof airfield, 2008
38 x 56 cm, watercolor

Wrong dimensioning: Milan, 2008
34 x 25 cm, pastel, sepia ink, watercolor, gray paper

Wrong dimensioning: Academy of Arts, Milan, 2008
25 x 34 cm, pastel, sepia ink, watercolor, gray paper

Wrong dimensioning: stairs of the Pinacoteca di Brera, Milan, 2008
34 x 25 cm, pastel, sepia ink, watercolor, pencil, gray paper

Sant'Andrea della Valle, Rome, 2008
40 x 29 cm, sepia ink, watercolor

Rome, 2008
51 x 67 cm, sepia ink, watercolor

Triumphal arch of Septimius Severus, Forum Romanum, Rome, 2008
42 x 62 cm, sepia ink, watercolor

Temple of Antoninus and Faustina, 2008
50 x 70 cm, sepia ink, watercolor

Rialto Bridge, Venice, 2008
40 x 60 cm, pastel, gray paper

Venice, 2008
60 x 40 cm, charcoal, gray paper

Venice, 2008
40 x 60 cm, charcoal, gray paper

Waters, 2009
32 x 54 cm, sepia ink, watercolor, pencil

Vertical composition of bridges and stairs,
infinitely growing, 2009
32 x 40 cm, pencil, Indian ink

Sunken City, 2009
38 x 55 cm, watercolor, Indian ink

Vertical composition of bridges and stairs, infinitely growing 4, 2009
32 x 40 cm, pencil, Indian ink

Windowsill, 2009
31 x 40 cm, watercolor, Indian ink, pencil

Saint Petersburg, snowy 2, 2009
31 x 40 cm, watercolor, Indian ink, pencil

Saint Petersburg, snowy 1, 2009
31 x 40 cm, watercolor, Indian ink, pencil

Polyptych: city window (upper left), 2009
27 x 19 cm, pastel, pencil, colored paper

Polyptych: city window (upper right), 2009
27 x 19 cm, pastel, pencil, colored paper

Polyptych: city window (lower left), 2009
27 x 19 cm, pastel, pencil, colored paper

Polyptych: city window (lower right), 2009
27 x 19 cm, pastel, pencil, colored paper

The Pantheon, Rome, 2009
25 x 35 cm, charcoal

Piazza San Pietro, Rome, 2009
25 x 35 cm, charcoal

View underneath the Colonnade of Piazza San Pietro, Rome, 2009
25 x 35 cm, charcoal

Basilica Maxentius, Rome, 2009
25 x 35 cm, charcoal

Brooklyn Bridge, New York City, 2009
27 x 19 cm, charcoal

Pan Am building, New York City, 2009
27 x 19 cm, charcoal

Fifth Avenue and Central Park, New York City, 2009
27 x 20 cm, charcoal

Wall Street and Trinity Church, New York City, 2009
27 x 20 cm, charcoal

Château de Blois, 2009
60 x 40 cm, watercolor, Indian ink

St. Gatien, Tours, 2009
60 x 40 cm, watercolor, Indian ink

235

The cathedral of Orléans, 2009
60 x 40 cm, watercolor, Indian ink

Château de Chambord: chimneys on the roof, 2009
60 x 40 cm, watercolor, Indian ink

Interior of the cathedral of Chartres, 2009
40 x 60 cm, watercolor, Indian ink

Campo San Moise, Venice, 2009
23 x 30 cm, watercolor

Santa Maria della Salute, Venice, 2009
31 x 23 cm, watercolor

Santa Maria della Salute, Venice, 2009
33 x 25 cm, charcoal

Fantasy drawing for the project of the Museum for Architectural Drawing or: Evolution of form 3, 2010
53 x 34 cm, charcoal

Fantasy drawing for the project of the Museum for Architectural Drawing or: Evolution of form 2, 2010
60 x 40 cm, charcoal

Fantasy drawing for the project of the Museum for Architectural Drawing or: Evolution of form 1, 2010
40 x 60 cm, charcoal

A museum, 2010
41 x 32 cm, charcoal

Sergei Tchoban

09.10.1962
Born in St. Petersburg, Russia

1980–1986
Earned degree at the Russian Academy of Arts, St. Petersburg

1986–1990
Practical work as graduate architect in Russia (since 1989 as freelance architect)

since 1992
commenced work with Nietz, Prasch, Sigl Architekten BDA, Hamburg, Germany

since 1995
Founding partner of nps tchoban voss Architekten BDA Hamburg, Berlin, Dresden; head of the Berlin branch
Member of the American Society of Architectural Illustrators (ASAI)

2004
Foundation of the architectural studio tchoban & partners in Moscow

2009
New member of the advisory council for urban design of the city of Linz, Austria
Launch of the S. Tchoban Foundation. Museum for Architectural Drawing, Berlin

Buildings (selection)

2009
Adina Hotel, new construction, Platz vor dem Neuen Tor 6, Berlin

Stuttgarter Platz 1, refurbishment and extension of a business building, Berlin

European Embankment, master plan, St. Petersburg

E plus, E-Plus-Strasse, new headquarters for a mobile phone net provider, Düsseldorf

2008
House by the Sea, new residential complex, Martinov Embankment, St. Petersburg

Corpus 25/Orangerie, refurbishment of an office building on the Polustrovo property, St. Petersburg

Müllerstrasse 36, new commercial and office building, Berlin

Titania-Palast, remodelling and refurbishment of retail areas of an historical monument, Berlin

2007
Department store at the Europa-Center, Tauentzienstrasse 9, Berlin

Synagogue Münstersche Strasse, remodelling of a former transformer station, Berlin

Business center Benois, refurbishment of a commercial and office building, Piskariovsky Prospect, St. Petersburg

2006
Business center Langenzipen, refurbishment of a commercial building, Kamennoostrovsky Prospect, St. Petersburg

C&A, new administrative headquarters, Wanheimer Strasse 70, Düsseldorf

Berolinahaus, remodelling of a commercial and business building, Alexanderplatz 1, Berlin

2005
Kurfürstendamm 38/39, new commercial and office building, Berlin

Refurbishment of a commercial and office building on Unter den Linden 32-34, Berlin

2004
City Quartier DomAquaree, hotel, residential and office buildings, Karl-Liebknecht-Strasse/Spandauer Strasse, Berlin

Tauentzienstrasse 18, new commercial and office building, Berlin

Wilmersdorfer Strasse 121, new commercial and office building, Berlin

Kurfürstendamm 64/65, refurbishment of a commercial and office building, Berlin

Berliner Vorstadt, master plan for a residential quarter, Potsdam

Riem-Arcaden, new city quarter and shopping center, Munich

Polustrovo, master plan on the former Rossija property, St. Petersburg (revised 2007)

2003
Kronprinzenkarree, office block and loft building, Reinhardtstrasse 48–52, Berlin

Osthafen, master plan on the Spree River, Berlin

2002
Kontorhaus Novalisstrasse, new commercial and office building, Berlin

Kurfürstendamm 42/Mommsenstrasse 71, remodelling of a commercial building, Berlin

2001
Cubix, new multiplex movie theater, Rathausstrasse 1, Berlin

Leipziger Platz Carré, masterplan, Berlin

2000
Kleine Rosenstrasse 14, remodelling of a commercial building, Hamburg

Alfred-Döblin-Haus, remodelling of the façade, Alexanderplatz 6, Berlin

1999
Stern Center, new shopping center and residential building, Potsdam

1998
Art Gallery Arndt (AEDES Gallery Extension), conversion of a transformer station, Rosenthaler Strasse 40/41, Berlin

1997
Java Tower, conversion of a coffee roasting factory, Langenhorner Chaussee 384, Hamburg

HGH Fragrance Resources, remodelling of the entrance and lobby, Borstelmannsweg 169, Hamburg

Current projects (selection)

nhow Design Hotel, Berlin, completion in 2010

Business Center Stephankiez, Berlin, completion in 2010

LSW, Wolfsburg, completion in 2011

Federation Tower Moscow City, Moscow, completion in 2009

Expo-Gate trade fair center, St. Petersburg, completion in 2010

Newskij City Hall, St. Petersburg, completion in 2012

Awards

2008
House of the Year 2009, Award of the Public of St. Petersburg, Organizer: Project Baltia (House by the Sea, St. Petersburg)

Gold Diploma of the Architects' Association of Russia, category: Best Realized Project (House by the Sea, St. Petersburg)

Gold Diploma of the Architects' Association of St. Petersburg, category: Best Realized Project (House by the Sea, St. Petersburg)

St. Petersburg Commercial Real Estate Awards – 2008, category: Best Office Building Class A (business center Langenzipen, St. Petersburg)

2005
Deutscher Natursteinpreis 2005, noted with destinction (City Quartier DomAquaree, Berlin)

2004
Silver Diploma of the Zodchestvo Festival 2004, Moscow, project: Best Architectural Objects 2002–2004, category: Project (House by the Sea, St. Petersburg)

2003
ArchMoscow 2003, Critics' Prize for the Best Foreign Entry (onsite architectural exhibition: B.A.U. Idee-Prozess-Raum)

2001
Deutscher Innenarchitekturpreis 2001 (Cubix movie theater)

2000
Architecture & Design Fair Moscow 2000, Reviewers' Award (onsite exhibition: Space for Art)

1999
BDA Hamburg Architekturpreis, 2nd place (Trabrennbahn Farmsen, Hamburg)

1998
Deutscher Städtebaupreis, honourable mention (Trabrennbahn Farmsen, Hamburg)

1995
Three times elected The World's Best 50 Architectural Perspectivists, by the editors of *Architecture in Perspective*, volumes 1, 2, 3, United States of America

1995–2008
Several Awards for Excellence of the International American Society of Architectural Perspectivists for architectural drawings

Exhibitions (selection)

2010

Architectural Worlds. Sergei Tchoban – Draftsman and Collector. Deutsches Architekturmuseum DAM, Frankfurt/Main, January 2010, catalogue

2009

Europa Kai – The new Dance Theater Quarter of St. Petersburg. Aedes Pfefferberg, Berlin, August 2009, catalogue

Die Wiederentdeckung Sretenkas (The Re-Discovery of Sretenka). AedesLand, Berlin, July 2009, design, participation, catalogue

AQUA. Galleria Antonia Jannone, Milan, Italy, January 2009, catalogue

2008

Berlin Moscow. Sochi Art Museum, September 2008

Sergei Tchoban – Zeichnen Planen Bauen. Exhibition under the patronage of the Mayor of the City of Dresden in line with the city's partnership bonds with St. Petersburg. Gebäudeensemble Deutsche Werkstätten Hellerau, June 2008

Architekturachse Russland Deutschland. Integration der deutschen Baukunst in die moderne Architektur von Sankt-Petersburg. Exhibition in line with the cultural forum Deutsche Woche in St. Petersburg 2008. Bronze Hall of the Architects' Association St. Petersburg, April 2008

2007

Architecture for the City. Peter Schweger and Sergei Tchoban. Academy of the Arts of Russia, St. Petersburg

XII. International Exhibition of Architecture and Design, ArchMoscow, Moscow, participation

2006

P. Schweger S. Tchoban – Federation Tower. DAZ, Berlin and Frankfurt/M

2005

Berlin-Moscow Moscow-Berlin – New Projects by S. Tchoban. Aedes Architecture Gallery, Berlin

Playground. Exhibition at the ArtPlay Architecture and Design Centre, Moscow, participation

P. Schweger. S. Tchoban. Federation Tower. The State Shussev Museum of Architecture, Moscow

2004

The Moscow Archeology of Sergei Tchoban. The State Shussev Museum of Architecture, Moscow

2003

New Architecture in Berlin. The State Shusev Museum of Architecture, Moscow, catalogue, curator and participation

STADTanSICHTEN – Planschrank Moskau (Visions for Moscow). ifa-Gallery, Berlin, Bonn, Stuttgart, concept and realization

Berlin im Fluss. Exhibition (participation) at the State Shussev Museum of Architecture, Moscow

50 Projects of the new Berlin. Exhibition at the State Shussev Museum of Architecture, Moscow, under the protectorate of the Senate of Berlin, curator and participation

2000

Space for Art. Exhibition during the ArchMoscow, organisation, concept, curator and participation, catalogue.

1999

Five Hand-drawn Worlds, Aedes Architecture Gallery, Berlin, catalogue, participation

1997

Java Tower, Aedes Architecture Gallery, Berlin, catalogue

List of Works